Old MacDonald Had a Farm

Written by Catherine Baker

Illustrated by Lee Holland

Collins

2

3

4

6

8

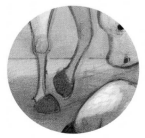  

9

10

12

13

Who lives on the farm? Can you make their sounds?

 Review: After reading

Read 1: Decoding

- In this book, there are opportunities to explore the sounds from the song "ee, igh, ee, igh, oa". Look for objects the words for which contain the sounds. (e.g. *tree, coat, mice*)
- Together, look for objects in the pictures that make sounds. (e.g. *the animals, water, a radio, chopping wood, the wind, a tractor*)
- Look for opportunities to explore alliteration, by focusing on things in the pictures that begin with /f/ on pages 2–3, /m/ on pages 4–5, /d/ on pages 6–7, /h/ on pages 8–9, /l/ on pages 10–11 and words that contain the sound /e/ on pages 12–13.

Read 2: Prosody

- Encourage the children to hold the book and turn the pages.
- Look at the pictures together and ask the children how many animals they can spot.
- Encourage the children to talk about what is happening in each picture.

Read 3: Comprehension

- For every question ask the children how they know the answer. Ask:
  - Would you like to visit Old MacDonald's farm? Why?
  - Which is your favourite picture? Why?
  - Do you think the mouse was naughty to take all those things, or do you think she was just trying to feed her babies and keep them safe?